Decorative Stained Glass Designs

38 Patterns for Beautiful Windows and Doors

Louise Mehaffey

STACKPOLE
BOOKS

To my very tolerant family

Copyright ©2013 by Stackpole Books

Published by
STACKPOLE BOOKS
5067 Ritter Road
Mechanicsburg, PA 17055
www.stackpolebooks.com

Printed in the United States of America

10 9 8 7 6 5 4 3 2 1

FIRST EDITION

Cover design by Wendy Reynolds

Library of Congress Cataloging-in-Publication Data

Mehaffey, Louise.
    Decorative stained glass designs : 38 patterns for beautiful windows and doors / Louise Mehaffey. — First edition.
        pages cm
    ISBN 978-0-8117-1144-9 (pbk.)
    1. Glass painting and staining—Patterns.   I. Title.
TT298.M423   2013
748.5028'2—dc23
                                                                2012036145

Contents

Introduction

In this book you'll find a compilation of thirty-eight original designs for stained glass windows that I created over a period of thirty years. This book is for those with experience in making stained glass windows, so I do not discuss the process. The designs are all original, developed and copyrighted by me. I provide the patterns for each panel, with photographs of my finished work and notes on making them.

I started working with stained glass in the early 1970s. My family had moved into a house with a really ugly plastic sidelight by the front door, and I decided to make a stained glass window to replace it. I started learning about this art, but before I could finish the window, we moved again. Nevertheless, I made the window and this experience was enough to hook me. I have been working with glass ever since. In 1998, I also started lampworking, and in recent years I've been focusing on that small-scale glass craft, so now I've decided to make my favorite stained glass designs available for other glass crafters to use.

My favorite part of working with stained glass was creating the designs. Over the years, I explored sandblasting and painting on glass, always incorporating that into my designs. Most of my business was making windows for homes, and it was always a challenge to create a design that satisfied both me and my client. Sometimes I was asked to do a commission that involved aspects with which I was not familiar, and I usually accepted those commissions. They forced me to learn new skills and led to some of my best designs. I also spent time every year creating designs just for me, and some of these designs led to working with more clients. I am not sure which I preferred, making a window for a client or making one just for me. They each had their limitations but also their freedoms. When making a window for a client, the design had to complement its location, and the style and subject were usually de-cided by the client. I found myself creating patterns I probably would not have designed otherwise, which was exciting, but I had to keep in mind what the client desired. When making a window for me, I was limited mainly by size, since I carried these around with me to exhibitions and shows, but I was free to create any design I wanted.

I used copper foil whenever feasible. This made the panels much lighter, which was important because of carrying them to shows. I could also cut and grind all the glass pieces of a design, put them in a box, and carry that around, so I could work on foiling the pieces when-ever I had the chance. This was certainly not ideal, but I was able to get much more work done that way. Using copper foil also enabled me to achieve more detail than lead came would have, although some came en-thusiasts may argue that point. I typically used a black-backed copper foil, because I often used a black patina on the solder lines, and the copper-colored back of the foil seen through the transparent glass would have detracted from the design.

Craftsmanship was very im-portant to me, and I worked to make the solder lines smooth on both the front and back, so that they didn't distract from the de-

This photo was the basis for the drawing on the next page. I liked the shape of the leaves, almost a pyra-mid with a burst of color at the top.

sign. Whenever I finished soldering a window, I cleaned it well, and then usually used a black patina on the solder. I felt that the bright silver solder lines distracted from the design, and using black patina made the design and the glass become the focus. It also eliminated that "brand new" element. When making autonomous panels, I used a strong zinc came for the outside edges, usually ½ inch, and I used a special patina for zinc so that became dark also. Because many people move so often now, some clients didn't want the window installed. They planned on hanging it in front of the current window so that they could easily take it with them when they moved. For these panels, I also used a strong zinc came. For panels that were being installed, I used ½-inch H lead came, because the outer edge could be easily trimmed to fit the opening. As a final task, I waxed both sides with a carnuba wax, which helped repel fingerprints and dust.

Learn about reinforcing your windows. Nothing is more discouraging than getting a phone call from a previous client telling you their window is sagging or buckling. Glass is very heavy and gravity is a strong force. It may take years, but if your windows are not properly reinforced, they will eventually sag, so learn to counteract it.

This drawing became the design for the window on page 48. I illuminated most of the background, focusing on the leaves and blossoms.

I developed many patterns, with my inspiration coming mainly from the natural world. I loved the lines in nature that meandered and looked effortless. Those lines are far from effortless to create in glass, but I enjoyed the challenge. Occasionally, a client wanted a more traditional design, so I developed some of those too. It was always a thrill to finish a window and see it in place, with natural light illuminating it. I was always fascinated by how the window changed as the light changed and by the reflection of the colors into the room. Stained glass is so dynamic! After all my years of creating patterns, I decided it was time to share them. I hope you use them as inspiration to create your own designs.

I thank my clients, who allowed me into their homes and trusted me to create something special for them. They often pushed me to stretch my skills, which led to some wonderful designs. Thanks also to my editor, Kyle Weaver, and Stackpole Books for allowing me to share my designs.

Using the Patterns

For each design, I provide the dimensions for the original window I made, but you can adapt the design to the size you want. To use the patterns in this book, make copies of the designs, enlarging them to whatever size you need. An autonomous panel is easier than installation in an opening, because the size doesn't have to be exact. Simply solder hooks onto the frame and add a chain to hang it. To create a

window to install, carefully measure the opening, enlarge the pattern to the largest measurement, and then decide where to trim the pattern to fit the smaller dimension. Another method of enlarging the design is to draw a grid on the pattern and then transfer the design to a larger grid. You can also simply sketch the design to the correct size.

Some Notes on Designing

I think of a stained glass pattern as a line drawing. The lines are the lead cames or copper foil lines, and the glass provides the color and shading. In many ways, it is like painting with light and color.

The number one thing you can do to design great windows is to draw. Take drawing classes, carry a sketchbook with you, and draw every day. Study lines, color, and composition. Don't draw stained glass designs, just draw. If you have been making stained glass windows for a while, this can be harder than it sounds. Forget about lead lines and just draw.

Carry a camera with you and take photographs when you can't make a sketch of something that catches your eye. (I am not a great photographer; I am only trying to document the subject for reference, not take a great photograph.) When you have a photo you want to translate into stained glass, first make a drawing—not a pattern but a drawing with shading, ignoring lead lines. When you have a drawing you like, translate that into a line drawing, and then work on creating a stained glass design. Now pay

attention to the shapes created by the lines, because you need to be able to cut those shapes from glass. As you work on this, be sure the pieces have a variety of sizes, some large and some small. Don't let your skill in cutting glass determine the design, rather make the glass express your design. Add lead lines when necessary for cutting glass, but try to keep them to a minimum, and have them reflect the style of your design. If the lines of your design are organic, let them meander to the edge rather than drawing a straight line to the border.

Designs can come from many places. While set up for an outdoor show one autumn, I kept looking at a crab apple tree near me. The red crab apples were a

Crab Apples detail

Nouveau Tree I (top) and Nouveau Tree II (right)

wonderful contrast with the dark green leaves. On the color wheel, these are complementary colors and I thought it would make a great design for a window. I borrowed a camera, took a roll of photographs (this was before digital cameras), and designed the crab apple window on page 20 from those photographs. That led to a commission for a cabinet door and also a circular window. Often, a successful design leads to several versions of that design. I took many other photographs that became designs, and I even used doodles to develop designs. Sometimes I simplified a design when I fabricated it again. The first Nouveau Tree (page 42) I made was larger and more complicated than the second one (page 44). The simplified version was faster and easier to fabricate, but don't let that dictate your design. The primary consideration should always be the design.

Learn techniques such as painting on glass, sandblasting, and fusing to expand your knowledge and use these tech-

niques to achieve the effect you want in your work. These techniques should not overpower your design, but be an appropriate and integral part of your window.

In some designs, it is important to have all the lead lines meet evenly. If the lines in the Ohio Star quilt design (page 78) did not meet correctly, it would be very obvious. This is

true in most traditional designs. In botanical designs, having every line meet another line evenly can make the design static. To avoid this, I sometimes used copper foil to extend design lines. Look at the Ivy Fence designs (pages 32 and 34) as an example of this. A few of the vines extend partway into a fence board. I also sometimes varied the width of the foil lines, either by using different widths of foil or trimming the foil with a knife. This was a subtle but effective way to add movement to a design.

Occasionally, I used tinned copper wire in an appropriate gauge to create details that would be very difficult to achieve with glass pieces. Tinned copper wire solders well and accepts any patina the same as the solder lines. If you can't find tinned wire, you can tin it yourself by applying flux to the copper wire and then adding solder. Be sure to hold the wire with pliers or another tool, be-

Ohio Star detail

Ivy Fence I detail

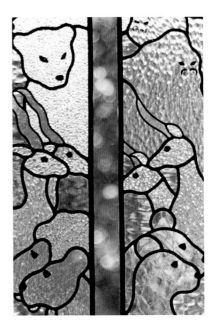

Ivy Fence II detail *Sampler Quilt detail* *Noah's Ark III detail*

cause copper transfers heat very well. I used 14-gauge wire for the stems in the Crab Apple window (page 20), and 22-gauge wire for stamens for Amaryllis (page 16) and the Rhododendron designs (pages 46 and 48).

Some designs needed different details that I couldn't create with glass pieces or wire, so I learned to paint on glass. I had accepted a commission that had lettering in the design, and I couldn't think of an appropriate way of putting that lettering in the window. A class with Albinus Elskus introduced me to this art, and his book *The Art of Painting on Glass: Techniques and Designs for Stained Glass* was a wonderful addition to my reference library. The paints I used are the traditional vitreous paints that must be fired in a kiln to make them permanent. The color came from the glass, with the paint in black or brown simply adding details. In both Ivy

Fence designs (pages 32 and 34), I painted veins on the leaves. The eyes of the animals in Noah's Ark (page 74) are painted with highlights scratched out.

Even after learning to paint, some of my designs needed details that I couldn't yet achieve, so I learned to sandblast glass. To create pieces of glass with two colors, I used flashed glass (in most cases, a base of clear glass with a thin layer of another color on top), covered it with contact paper, and cut out the sections where I removed the color by sandblasting it away. This method created pieces of glass with both a solid color and clear frosted (sandblasted) sections, and enabled me to create the details in the King of Spades (page 92), Queen of Diamonds (page 94), and Carousel (page 90) designs. Some sections were made by sandblasting transparent glass, which created a "frosted" design; that didn't create two

colors, because the color of that glass is integral to the glass.

Once you have a pattern drawn, the overall size can often be changed simply by adding or changing the border or making it wider or narrower, although the size of the border needs to be appropriate for the design. I often used beveled glass to add a little sparkle, and 1-inch-wide bevels inside the outer border were great for setting off the center pattern. I thought of the glass border as the frame for the design. If you are framing your designs with wood, or installing them in an opening, then a glass border may not be needed.

Making the Pattern

When you have finished a design, lay out your pattern material (I often used poster board), cover it with carbon paper, and lay your design on top. Tape everything to the table so nothing moves while you are tracing. Trace each line and then number each piece. If you number each color in sequence, it will be easier to sort the pieces later; for example, number the green leaves sequentially, then the petals, then the background, etc. Also add an arrow to indicate the direction of any texture lines. After everything is traced, numbered, and has arrows, remove all the tape. If the design is relatively complex, before cutting the pieces apart, add a line of color to each piece. Sometimes I even added shading to the pattern pieces to make it easier to match it to the shading in the glass. Now use pattern shears to cut the pieces apart, and sort each color into a pile.

Choosing the Glass

Take your time choosing glass. This task is critical to the success of a window, and the more windows you create, the more you will be able to visualize the final result. Learn to recognize the different manufacturers of glass and become familiar with all their textures and colors. The color of the glass is very important, and if you are not familiar with color theory, take a class or do some reading. In addition,

the texture and the opacity are also very important. I often use both opaque and transparent glass in the same window, playing with the contrast between them. Desag semi-antique glass was one of my favorite choices for transparent background glass; it is available in beautiful colors and has a slight texture to it. For leaves and petals, I like glass that has color variations, and I use that variation to create the shading of the drawing. The shading and arrow on the paper pattern piece helped to place it on the glass to achieve the proper shading of the glass. This took extra time, but the end result was worth it.

Because I am frugal, it is hard to cut a pattern piece from the middle of an expensive glass sheet to get the shading I want, but again, the result is worth it. It helps to have a lightbox so you can see the glass with light behind it, because many sheets of glass look very different with light coming through them. In a pinch, sit pieces of glass on a windowsill. You can also rig up a lightbox by using two stools or boxes set 24 inches or more

apart with a piece of clear glass over them and a light on the floor. You can then lay the stained glass on this to get an idea of how it will look with light behind it. Look at all the glass for that design to be sure it all works together. I also tried to visualize how much of each type of glass would be in the final panel. Some strong colors or textures can overwhelm the design.

The glass you choose can dramatically alter the appearance of a window. If I repeat a design, I sometimes change the glass, often to improve it but sometimes just because I want to use another glass. I also sometimes changed the pattern as I was cutting pieces. Don't think that because you have a finished design it is etched in stone. You are free to make improvements as you cut and fabricate your design.

After I finished a window, I always studied it—what worked well, and what could I have done to make it better? Learn to critique your own work. This is difficult, but well worth the effort. It is how you will learn and grow.

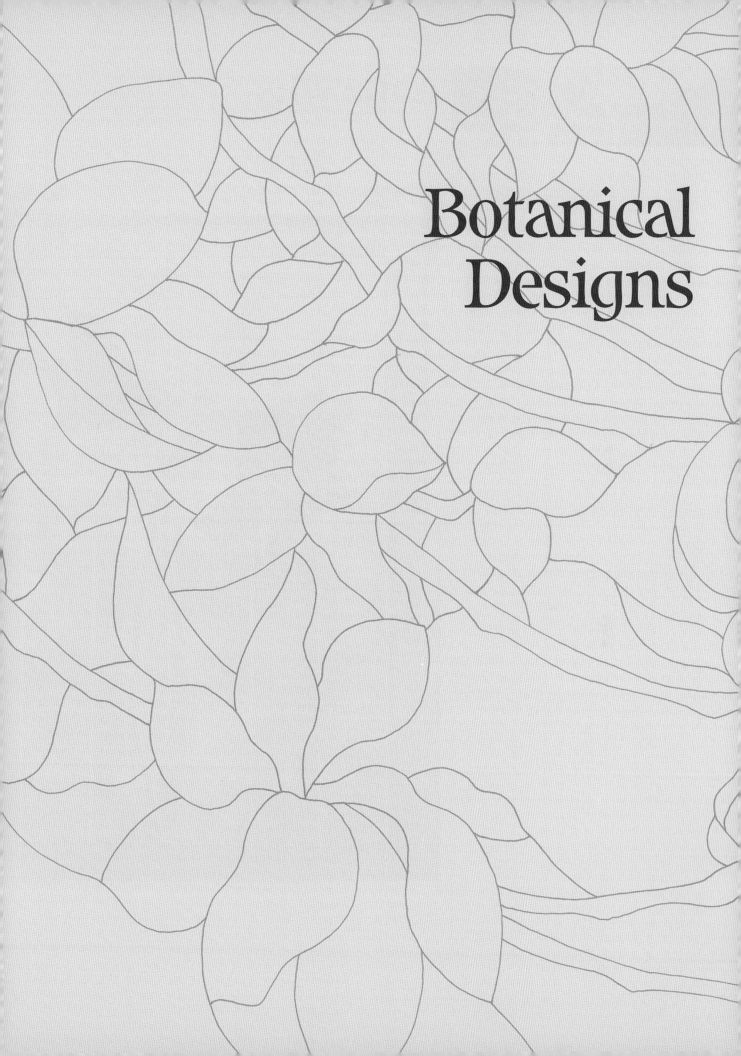

Botanical
Designs

Amaryllis

18 x 27 inches

A friend sent me an amaryllis bulb one Christmas, and when it bloomed, I was so impressed with the flowers that I decided to create a design with them. There was so much background in the design that I divided it into a grid, a purposely uneven grid. Some lines of the grid were placed to help with cutting the glass and some were placed as a design element. I had a sheet of a red/orange mottled glass that was a perfect color for the blooms. The first time I fabricated this design I used a pale green semi-antique glass for the background and a dark green semi-antique glass for the border, the same glass as the stems and leaves. I ultimately decided there was too much green in the panel, so the second time I fabricated it, I used a clear patterned glass for the background, and I thought this was more successful. To make the stamens, I bent the ends of pieces of 22-gauge tinned copper wire into a small rough circle, put a blob of solder on those ends, and shaped the wires like the stamens. Then I soldered the other ends to a seam in the flower.

Clematis

13 x 28 inches

While working on this design for a client, he brought me several clematis blossoms. They were totally wilted by then, but it was enough to inspire this panel. I used Youghiogheny stipple glass for both the flower petals and leaves and a deep purple for the flower centers. The glass for the flowers was mostly a rich purple hue, but had touches of pale blue and even red, which gave it vibrancy. The stipple glass had a wonderful quality of gathering the light and appearing to glow. The background was a very pale blue semi-antique glass. The design was originally hung in a transom, and several years later when they moved, I soldered hooks on one end so they could hang it in a window in their new house. The design worked in a vertical position also, and the client told me that the reflection of the window into the room looked like a natural vine.

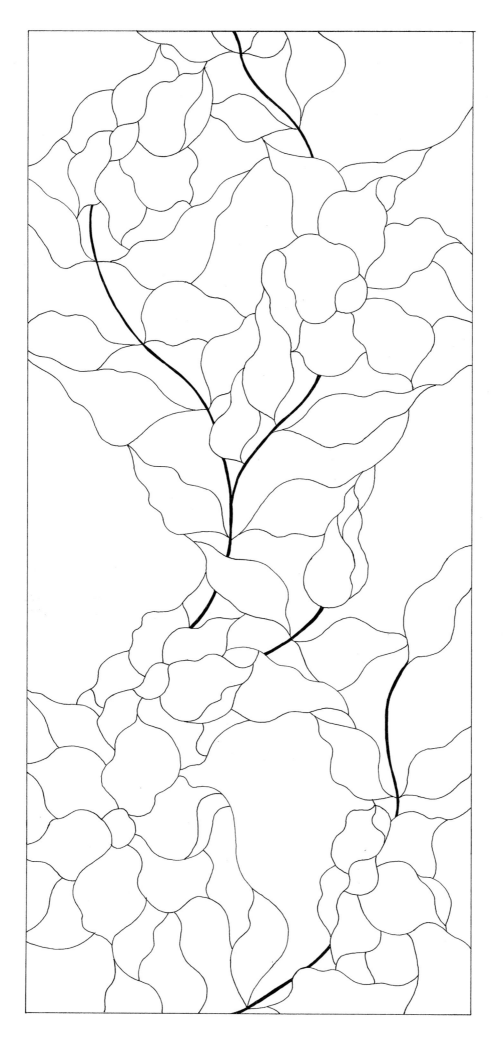

Crab Apples

24 x 32 inches

The branches could have been cut from a brown glass, but I thought that the solder on copper foil created a more interesting texture. To create the branch, I cut the glass pieces to meet each other, creating a surface on which to lay the foil. Then I taped foil on the glass for the branch and trimmed it with a knife. If you can find sheets of copper foil with a sticky back, that is great to use. If not, use the widest foil you can find and build the width you want, making sure to overlap and press all the edges down well. If there are open spaces, the solder will fall through the pieces, making it very difficult to get a nice texture on it, so overlap and press the foil edges well. Apply flux and solder. You will not be able to make a really smooth solder line on the wide foil, but I think the texture of the solder adds to the design. After fluxing and soldering this side of the window, turn it over. Tape and trim the branch on the back side and then flux and solder the back. Where the glass was transparent, I was especially careful to trim the foil the same as the front to conceal the back of the tape. I used 14-gauge tinned copper wire for the crab apple stems. For the leaves, I chose a green glass with a lot of color variation. The background is a clear semi-antique and the crab apples are a rich, antique red.

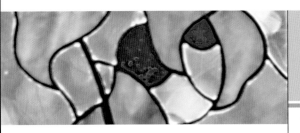

Crab Apples Cabinet Door

12 x 26 inches

A commission led to this adaption of the original design. It was inserted in a kitchen cabinet door. The client gave me the actual door, which made sizing the panel much easier. I chose this section of the larger design because there was so much vertical movement to match the vertical opening in the cabinet door, and I simplified the design because the size of this design was much smaller than the original one. Because I thought the glass I had chosen for the original crab apple design was so successful, I used the same glass here. The client was fine with being able to see into the cabinet so easily through the background glass; otherwise I would have used a clear textured glass to obscure the view.

Crab Apples Circle

18½ inches diameter

I really liked the crab apple design, but it was a large, complex panel that took many hours to complete. To simplify it a little, I adapted the design to a circle. I soldered hooks onto the outside lead, being careful to solder them into the panel itself for strength, and added a chain so it could easily be hung in a window. Many of my designs, because they are versatile, can be used as autonomous panels.

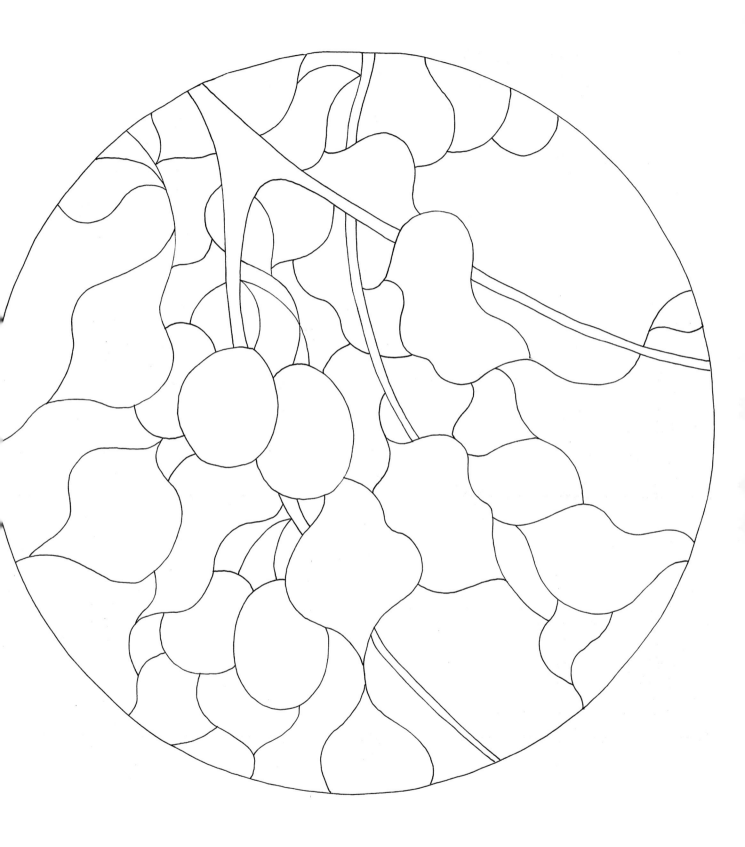

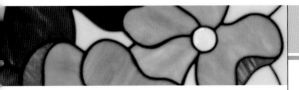

Dogwood

14³/4 x 36 inches

The blossoms of a dogwood tree in a neighbor's yard inspired this design. The client chose the blue glass for the petals, and because the glass didn't have much variation in color, I curved the edges of a few petals and used a much darker blue color to create depth. I used jewels for the centers of the flowers to add some sparkle. I also extended the design into the border in a few places. The client wanted the view through the window totally obscured, so I used a white opaque background.

Forest Primeval

19 x 24 inches

This design was the result of a doodling, which I shaded and developed into this pattern. Using the glass to create the shading was important to the design, and I created depth by using both opaque and transparent glass. By using the transparent glass in places other than just the central section, I was able to create an illusion of narrow pillars. A glass border didn't seem appropriate, so I finished it with a wooden frame. This design was meant to be hung as an autonomous panel.

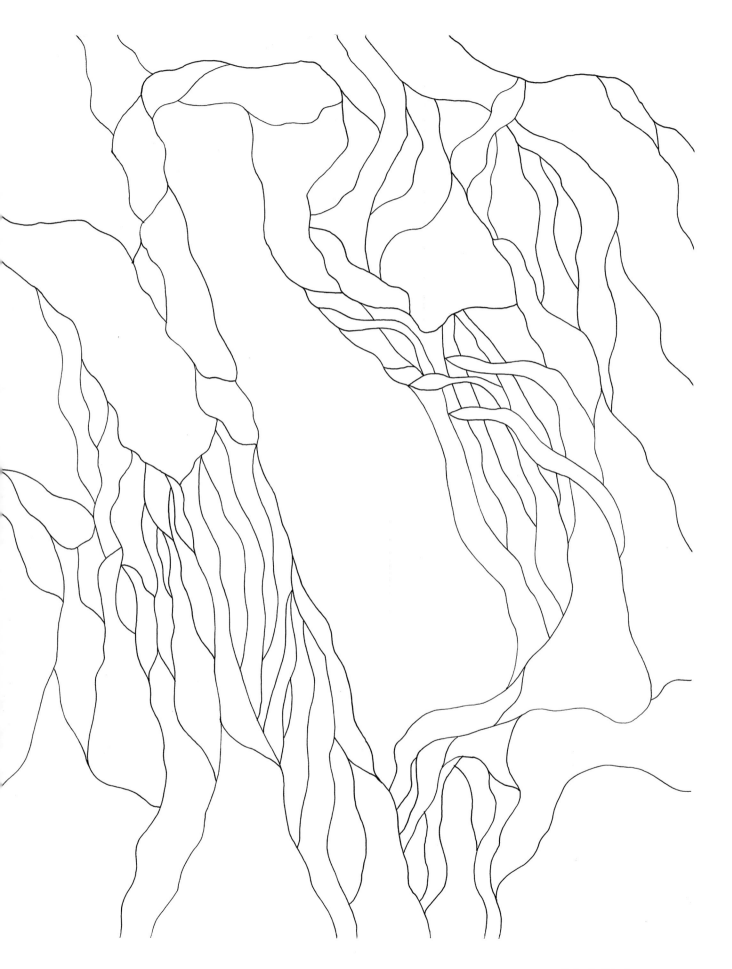

Iris (Dan's Door)

24 x 26½ inches

A friend opened a gallery and chose an iris as his logo. I made this window for the upper half of a wonderful swinging wooden door between the kitchen and dining room. A local restaurant had a bed of irises in bloom, so I took a roll of photographs and developed this design. I used a purple Youghiogheny stipple glass for the blooms and a clear textured glass for the background. I had a small sheet of pale lavender glass that complemented the purple blooms, and I used that around the circle; however, when I cut one of the pieces, a corner snapped off and I didn't have enough glass to cut another piece. After thinking about it, I cut the other corner off and inserted a round jewel. To balance that, I did the same on the top of the circle. This was a happy accident, because the jewels added some needed sparkle.

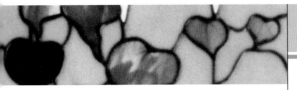

Ivy Fence I

25 x 24 inches

My backyard fence has ivy growing on it, and this design was made in early summer before the ivy covered the entire fence. Most of the vines are lead lines. To extend a few vines, I finished all the soldering and cleaned the glass well. Then I taped and burnished copper foil on the glass where I wanted to extend the ivy vines and trimmed it with a knife. I carefully fluxed the foil with as little flux as possible, soldered it, and cleaned it. If you work carefully, the foil should stay attached to the glass. If it comes loose, you can carefully put a tiny dab of glue to attach it again. I also painted and fired the veins in the leaves to add some detail. The pale blue transparent glass at the very top of the design was a nice contrast to all the opaque glass.

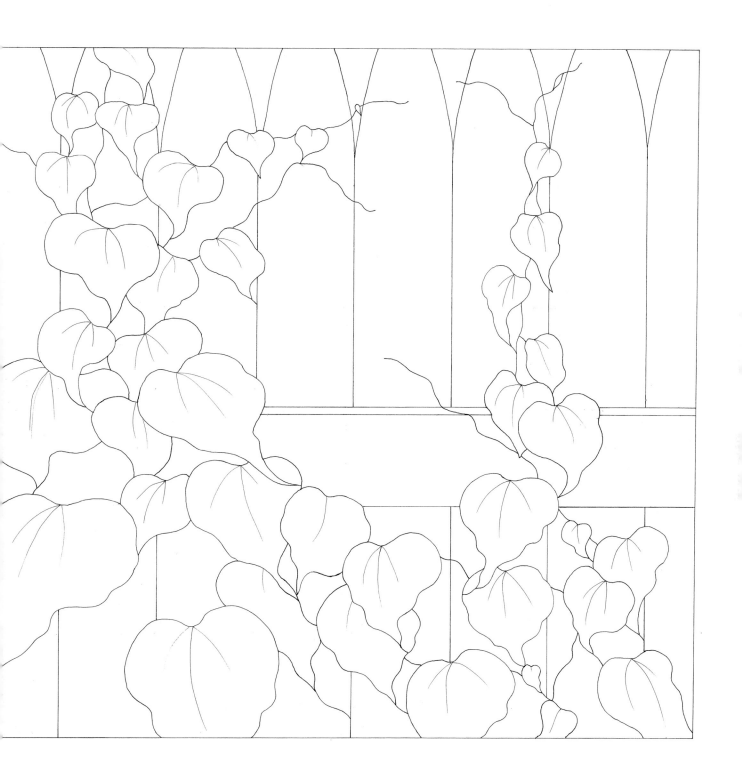

Ivy Fence II

20 x 36 inches

I adapted my first Ivy Fence design to fit a window in a bathroom. The clients wanted the window to block any view from the other side, even at night with the light on in the bathroom, and this opaque glass worked well. The pale transparent blue at the top was high enough to not be a problem. The amber glass worked well for the pattern and texture of the wooden fence. I again painted veins on the leaves to add definition.

Lucy II

17 x 25 inches

Lucy was my cat for more than eighteen years, and when she passed away, I created this design as a tribute to her. She had beautiful large green eyes, so to create them I first fused clear glass over dichroic glass cut to an approximate size. Then I cut and ground the eye pieces to the exact size, painted the pupils, and fired the pieces again. This firing was high enough to permanently fuse the black paint to the glass, but not high enough to change the shape of the glass. The fused dichroic glass created eyes with great depth and sparkle, but unfortunately they are very difficult to photograph. The black glass is semi-antique, which is a dark transparent black. I felt a black opaque glass would be too stark. I also painted and fired the whiskers to add details.

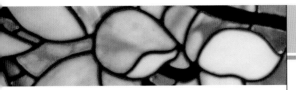

Magnolias

20¼ x 28½ inches

One year the weather must have been perfect for a huge magnolia tree in a neighbor's yard. The blooms were enormous and prolific, and I loved the movement of the branches and petals. After taking a roll of photographs, I chose one to use in developing a pattern. I hadn't realized until I drew the design that there is no green when the tree is blooming, just pink blossoms in many shades. I found a pink glass that had very pale to dark shades of pink, and the background is a semi-antique clear glass. Because of the large range of pink shades, the window didn't need another color.

Magnolias Octagon

20¾ x 20¾ inches

A client asked for a magnolia design for their octagon window, but they wanted a deeper pink than my original Magnolia design. It went in a bathroom window, so I used a heavily textured clear glass for the background. Because it was clear, it allowed a lot of natural light into the room, but the texture obscured vision. In two places, I extended the design into the border. When creating a design for an octagon window, I always made a template from heavy paper, because the shape was usually not a true octagon.

Nouveau Tree I

31 x 40¼ inches

Some friends who are potters commissioned me to create this design for an interior window. They wanted to be able to easily see through the window, so I used clear and very pale amber semi-antique glass for the background. I really liked the contrast between the semi-antique background glass and the opaque glass of the tree and leaves. The mottled glass of the tree and leaves added an interesting texture. The subject matter and the curves of the border are reminiscent of Art Nouveau designs.

Nouveau Tree II

18 x 29 inches

The first Nouveau Tree design was too large to carry around to shows, so I scaled it down and simplified the design. The colors are the same, although I used a different glass for the leaves and border. Compare this panel to the first Nouveau Tree, and you can see how glass choices affect the finished design.

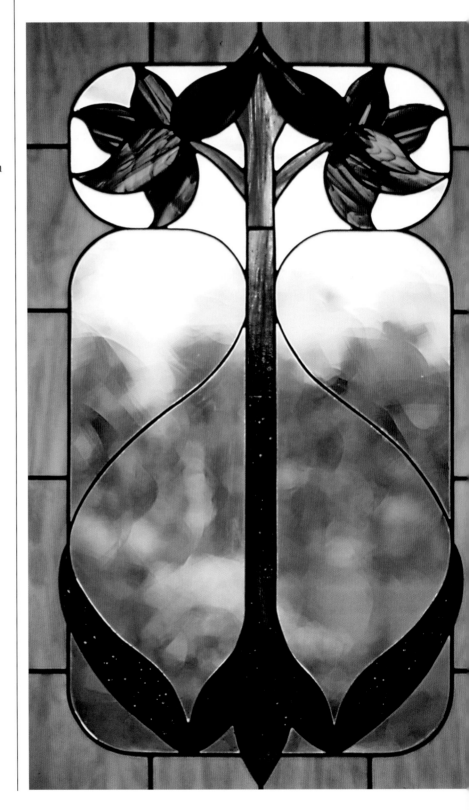

Rhododendron before the Rain

18½ x 22 inches

A huge rhododendron grows beside my front door, and it has inspired several designs, this one just before the blooms appeared. The color of the green leaves and the pale gray background glass had the saturation of color that occurs just before it starts to rain. The leaves were from a single sheet of glass with a wonderful variation, and the background was a very pale gray semi-antique glass. I used copper foil to create the segments on the buds instead of cutting each segment separately.

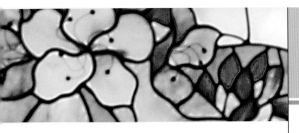

Rhododendron in Spring

24 x 24 inches

When my rhododendron bloomed, I created this design in an octagon shape. The first time I fabricated it, I used a green mottled glass for the leaves and a pale pink for the blooms, which I liked very much. But I couldn't decide on a glass for the outside border. I ultimately used a dark green glass. I wasn't totally happy with that, so I made another panel, this time using Youghiogheny stipple glass for the leaves and flowers and a variegated pink for the border. The stipple glass has a wonderful quality of gathering the light and glowing, making it appropriate for fresh, new growth. I thought this combination of glass was more successful. I added some stamens with 22-gauge tinned copper wire. The hooks for the chain extend into the soldered seams on the border.

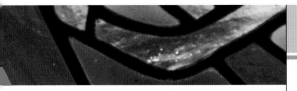

Roots

17½ x 24 inches

This design was the beginning of my botanical style. I had sketched the roots of a tree along a riverbank and later decided it would make an interesting window. I enjoyed creating the intertwined roots and using the glass to create the shading. The texture of the glass for the roots was a nice contrast to the semi-antique background. To finish it, I used a wooden frame.

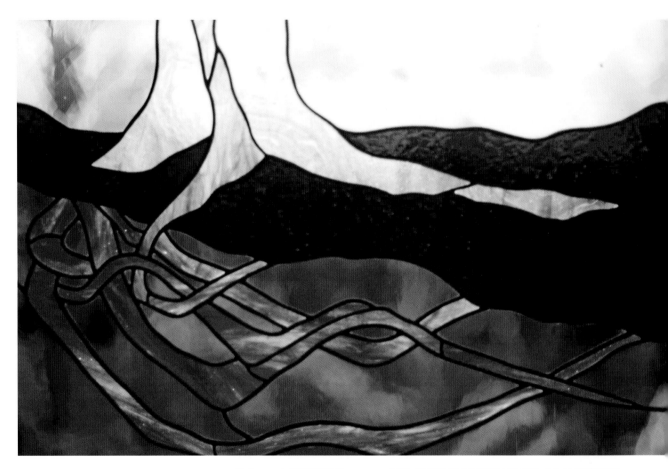

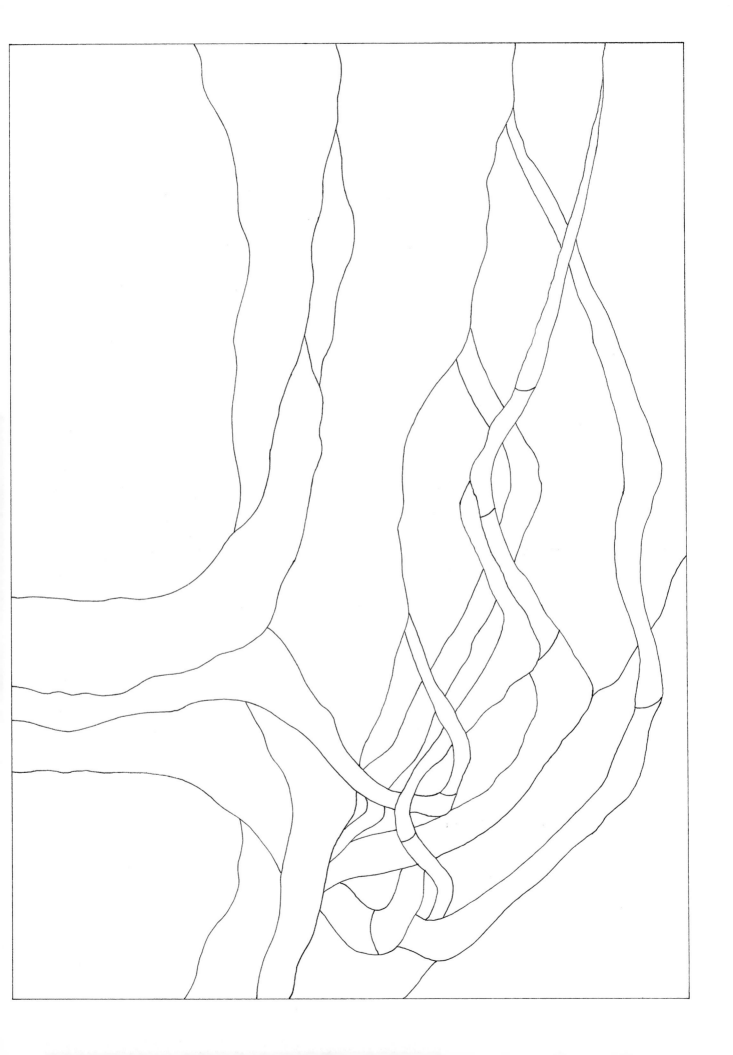

Rose in a Circle

14½ x 14½ inches

Roses are such beautiful flowers. I chose this one bloom to feature in a small autonomous panel. I have made it in different color combinations, but this was one of my favorites. The fracture streamer glass outside the circle complemented the flower so well, and I added an inner border of 1-inch beveled glass for a little sparkle.

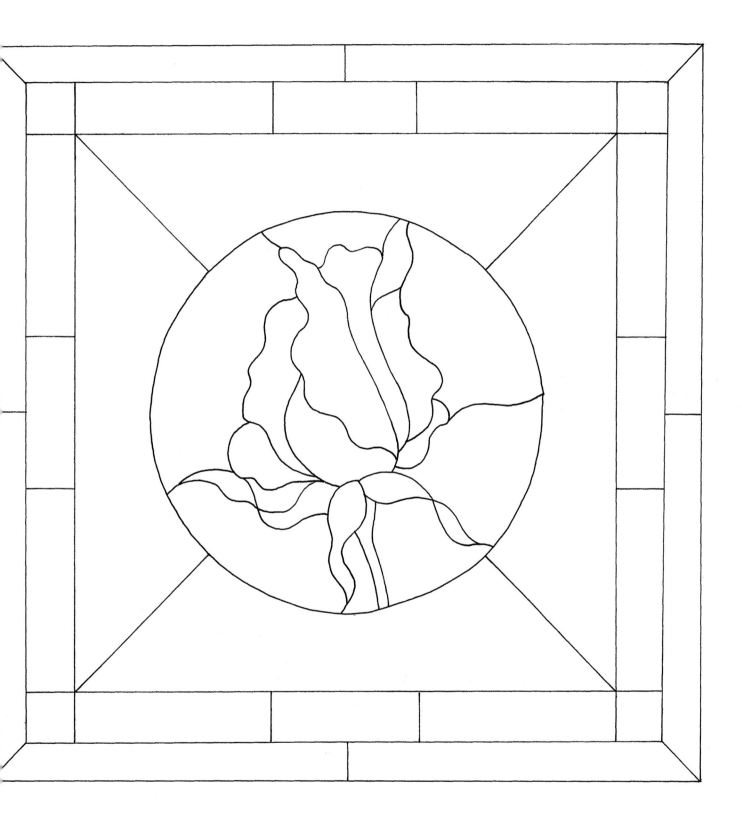

Trillium

10 x 17¾ inches

This small panel went in a diamond-shaped section of a window. Because of the unusual shape, I made a template of the window first and fabricated the panel to that size to be sure it fit. I had to research this flower, and I carefully chose the glass so it would be an accurate depiction. The semi-antique clear glass in the background added a little texture, which was much more interesting than using clear window glass would have been.

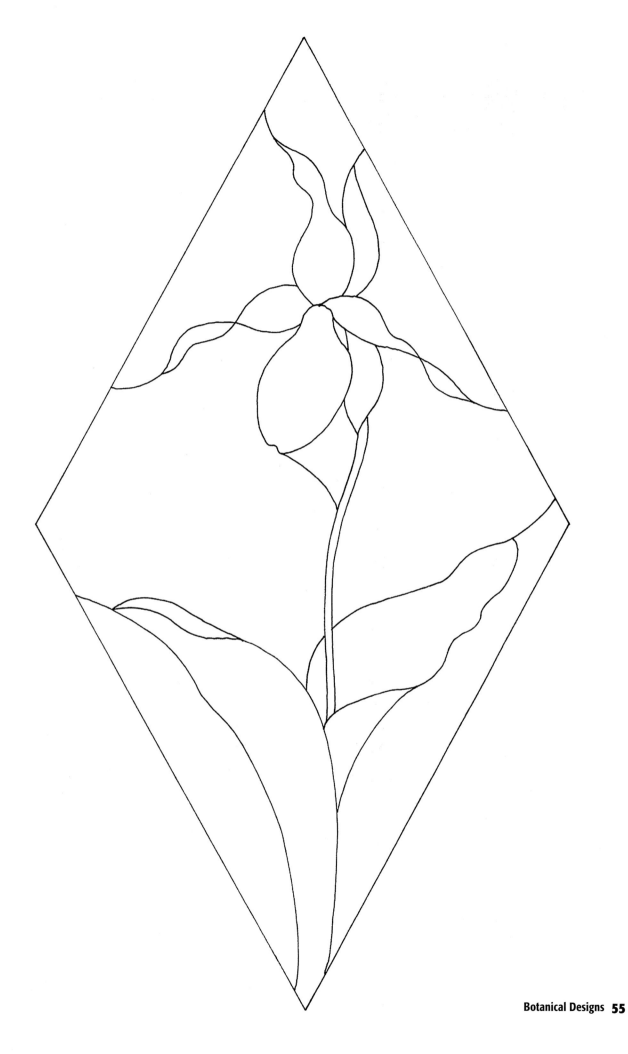

Violets

26 x 36½ inches

The purple and green color scheme is very striking. The glass for both the flowers and leaves had some color variation, which I used for shading. This panel was for a second-story window, so privacy was not an issue. The client did want the view obscured a bit, but wanted natural light to come through, so I used a seedy clear glass for the background. A 1-inch beveled glass inner border added some sparkle. The second time I fabricated the window, I scaled it down and used a different glass for the background, which obscured the view.

Wisteria

16 x 37¼ inches

This design was for a window beside a front door, and after researching the flowers, I used a simple trellis to wind the vines around. It was a convenient way to break up the vine into pieces that could be more easily cut and also added a needed contrasting color. The color choice was the client's, and I think it was successful, although I would probably have chosen a glass with more color variation for the flowers. The background is a wispy white. This allows some natural light in, but it can't easily be seen through.

Traditional Designs

Circles in a Border

23 x 32⅛ inches

This panel was installed in the upper half of a double-hung window, over a permanently installed air conditioner. The clients had been married for seven years, so I put seven circles down each side of the design. The circles were a more difficult design element than a straight-lined element, but it echoed the border in a rug in the room. The clients wanted the view obscured, so I used a heavily textured clear glass for the background, which still allowed light into the room, and opaque or dark transparent glass for the rest of the window. I used five borders in three colors, not counting the red circles, and varied the widths. This again echoed the rug, and the colors were chosen to coordinate with it. I really liked the effect of using many borders in different sizes and colors and used this design element in later windows. It can also be a way of increasing the size of the pattern, but be sure to keep the border an appropriate size for the design.

Three Cubes

13 x 16¾ inches

A friend gave me some house-shaped beveled pieces of glass, and after arranging and rearranging four of them with other beveled shapes, I decided I liked this layout. I used cobalt blue glass for the border and pale blue glass to contrast with the 2-inch beveled squares. Using different shades of the same color helped to unify the panel, and having diagonal lines in the corners instead of rectangular lines related to the diagonal lines of the three squares.

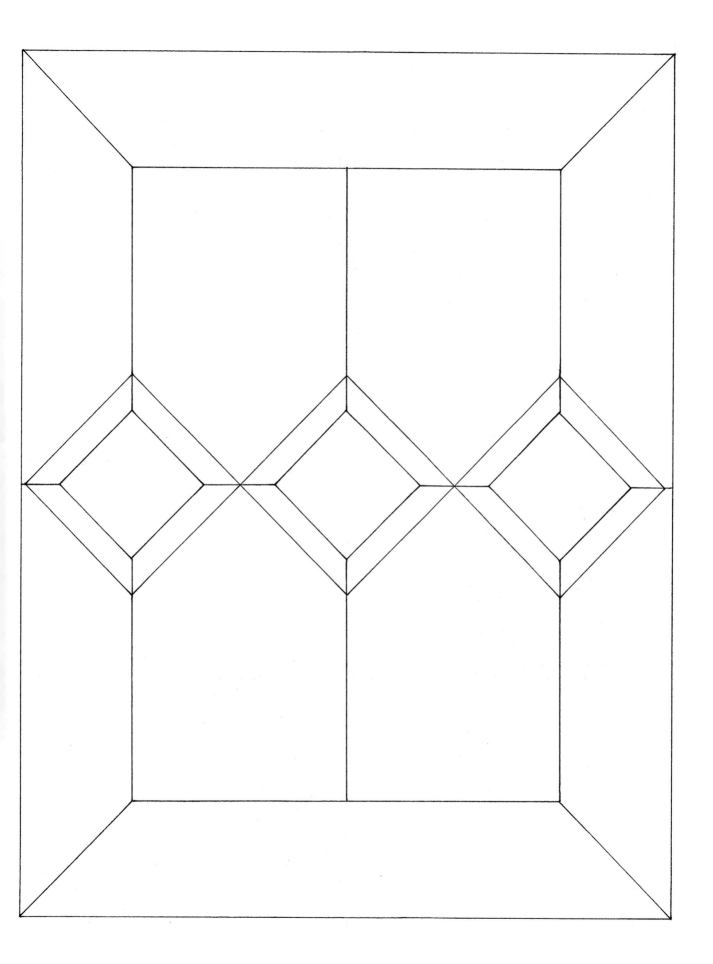

Three Hearts

14½ x 29 inches

A commission for a small transom led to this design. The client wanted beveled hearts and no colored glass. When working with beveled pieces, I usually trace the exact pieces to be used after I have the pattern drawn and before I cut any glass, because the pieces can vary in size. I used squares to widen the center motif and then added borders to reach the necessary size. The glue chip glass was a nice contrast to the clear bevels. This window allowed a lot of natural light into the room.

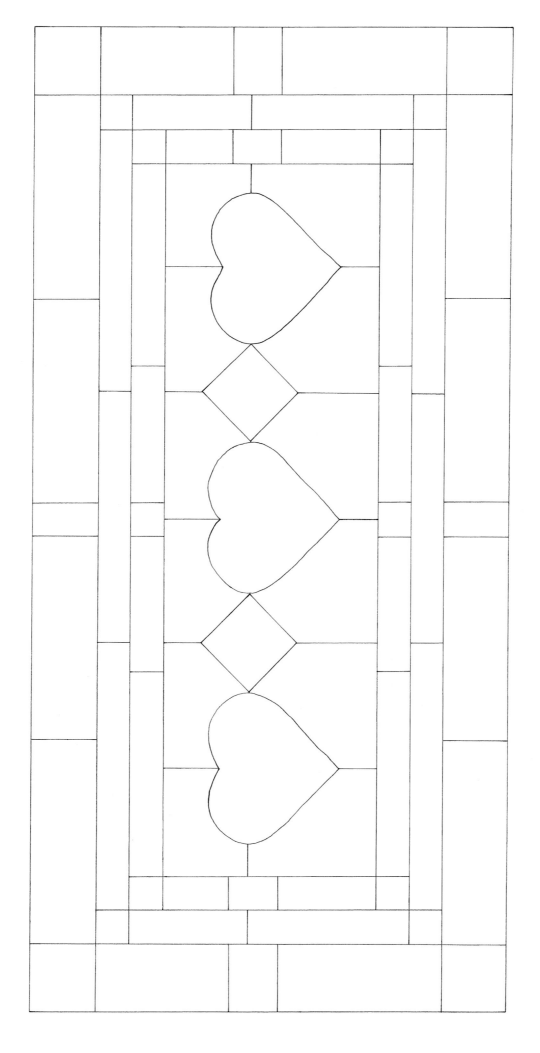

Victorian Arch

13 x 18½ inches

I fabricated this design several times, using different colors each time, and this blue-and-green combination was my favorite. The background was a very pale blue semi-antique glass. The design was inspired by Victorian windows, and I liked the idea of making an arched shape instead of a rectangle. When hanging the panel, I felt one hook at the top would allow the panel to turn, so I soldered two hooks where I could solder them into a seam for strength.

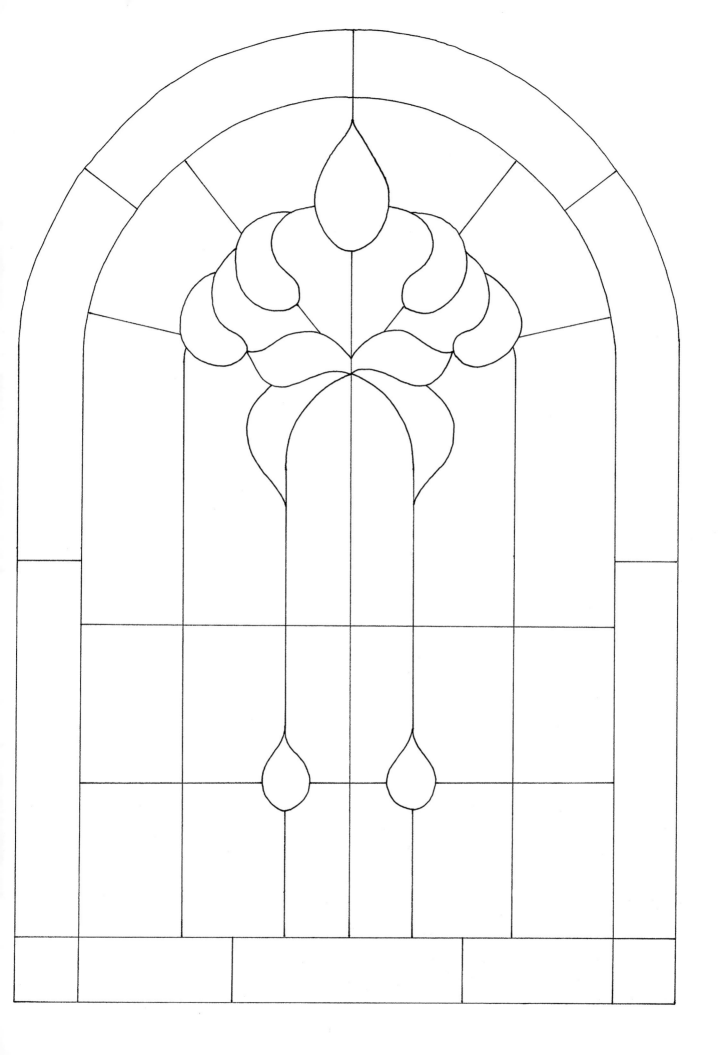

Special
Designs

Jacuzzi Window

35³/₄ x 24 inches

This design was a departure from my normal style. The clients wanted an abstract and modern design, and it was fun creating it. Even though it went in a window over a Jacuzzi, they wanted mostly transparent glass, so that they could see the beautiful view out the window. I used an opaque glass for the border and added just a few pieces of this in the design. I also used Cotswold glass in a few places as a contrast to all the smoother clear glass, along with beveled pieces in different sizes for sparkle.

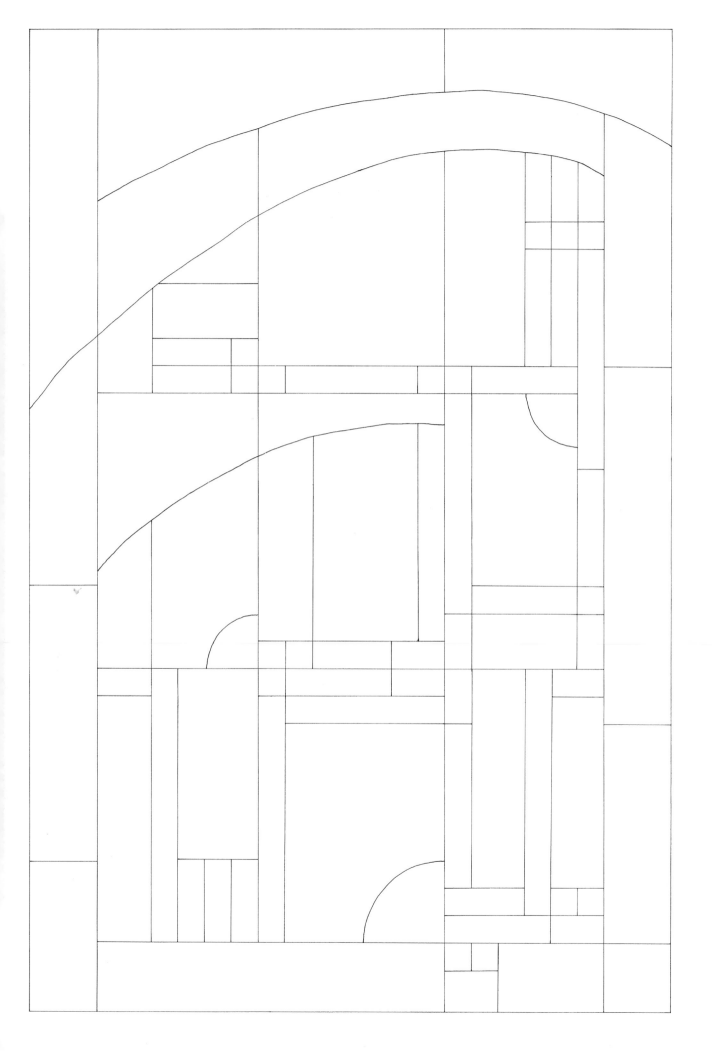

Noah's Ark I and II

6 x 62½ inches

The Noah's Ark I and II designs were a commission that I handled by phone and mail. While talking to the client on the phone, she described what she wanted: a Noah's ark theme with Noah, a rainbow, a dove, the ark, and of course animals. She had two narrow sidelights she wanted to fill, only 6 inches wide and 62 inches high. At first I thought this would be an impossible design, but before I finished talking to her, I had the basic idea. I worked on some rough sketches and mailed those and glass samples for her approval. If I had used shades of brown glass for the animals, the windows would have been very dark, so I used clear glass in many textures. The only color was a pale blue sky, the rainbow and the dove. I painted the olive branch in the dove's mouth, the figure of Noah on the ark, and the eyes of all the animals.

Left panel

Right panel

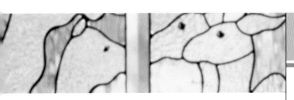

Noah's Ark III

19 x 39 inches

I really liked the Noah's Ark I and II designs, so I combined the two narrow panels into one panel and shortened the design by eliminating some animals. An inner border of 1-inch beveled glass separated the two designs, but I lined up the ark. The Cotswold glass in the outer border added a unifying frame.

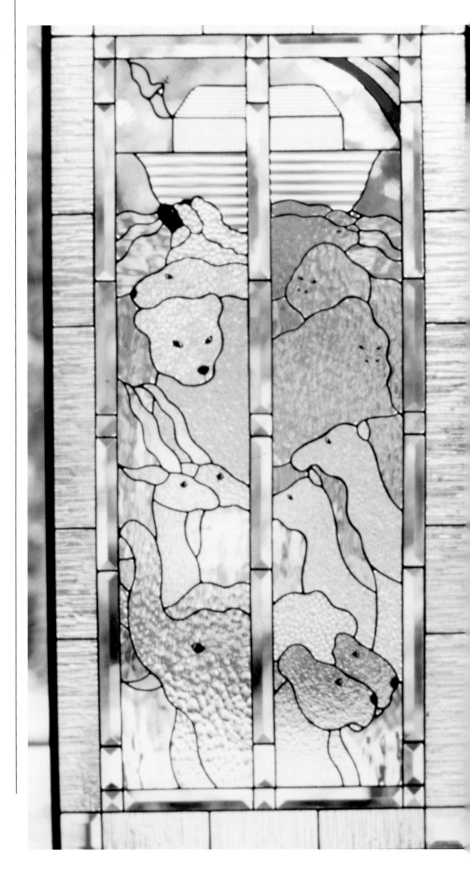

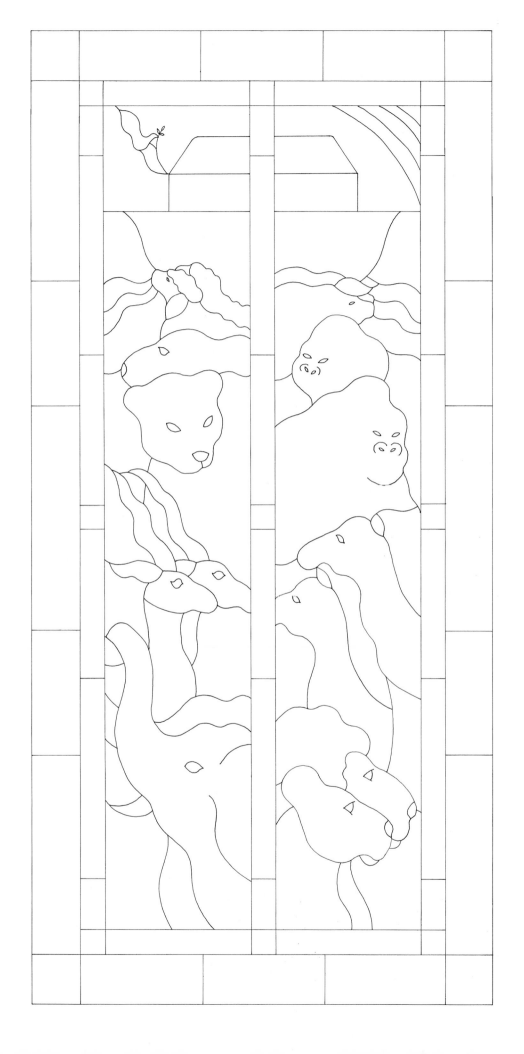

Ohio Star Quilt

16 x 16 inches

At one time in my life, I made quilts, so I decided to make a small autonomous panel of a quilt design. It was easy to cut the glass, because it was all straight lines; but if the lines of the glass pieces didn't match evenly, it would have been very obvious. I spent time trimming the foil to make sure the pieces matched. The clear glue chip glass was a nice contrast to the smooth texture of the semi-antique blue colors.

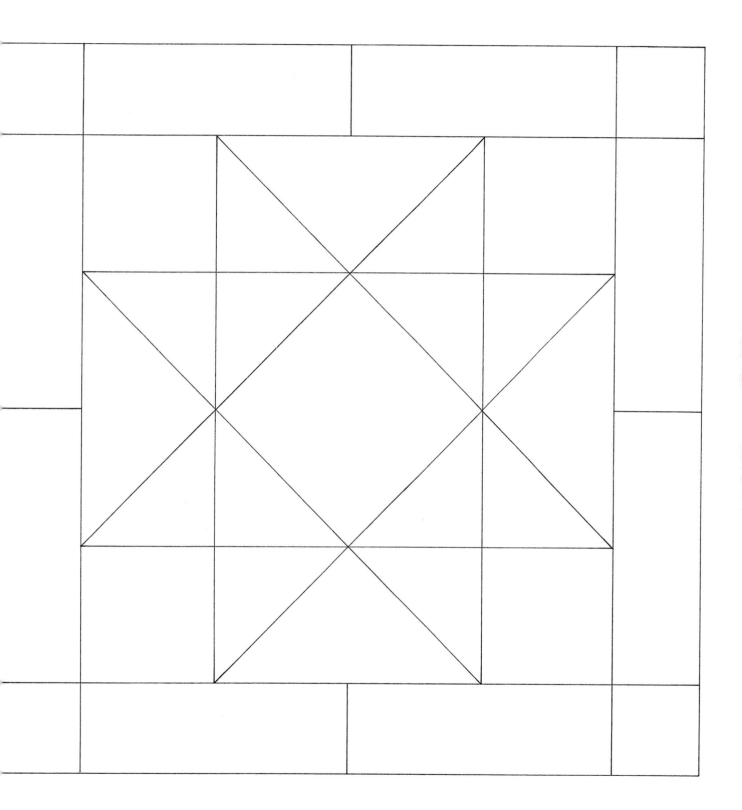

PRR
(Pennsylvania Railroad)

17 x 17 inches

A customer actually brought me the PRR sign so I could see exactly what he wanted. He was a collector of train memorabilia, so it was important that I made it correctly. I traced it so the panel was the same size as the sign. The colors were accurate, but I used a textured amber glass to add some interest. Hooks were soldered to the top, so it hangs as an autonomous panel.

Prairie I

8 x 37 inches

This style of work is also called Craftsman or Arts and Crafts. It is reminiscent of a more simple era, reflected in the deceptively simple straight lines. As in the Ohio Star Quilt panel, mismatched lines become very obvious, so the glass must be cut accurately. The panel was for a sidelight by a front door. The client did not want to be able to see through the window, so I used a heavily textured clear glass for the background. This allowed some natural light into the hall. The other colors were chosen to match those in an oriental rug.

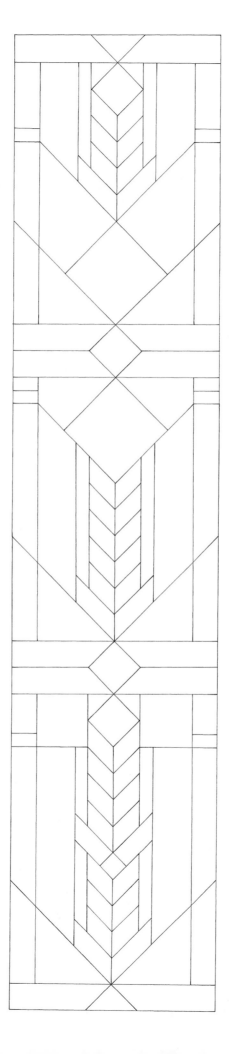

Prairie III

15 x 20 inches

I simplified the Prairie design and again used a heavily textured clear glass for the background. The color scheme was also simplified. The border was an opaque glass, which I also used in a few other places, and I used transparent glass for the rest of the design. The texture of the light mauve matched the texture of the clear background glass.

Sampler Quilt

20 x 20 inches

After I made the Ohio Star Quilt design, a friend who was a fabric quilter asked me to create a sampler quilt. I spent some time researching quilt designs, deciding which ones to use because the pattern had to be created with only two colors. Each pattern was sandblasted into flashed glass, and I used an opaque white glass to join the quilt patterns.

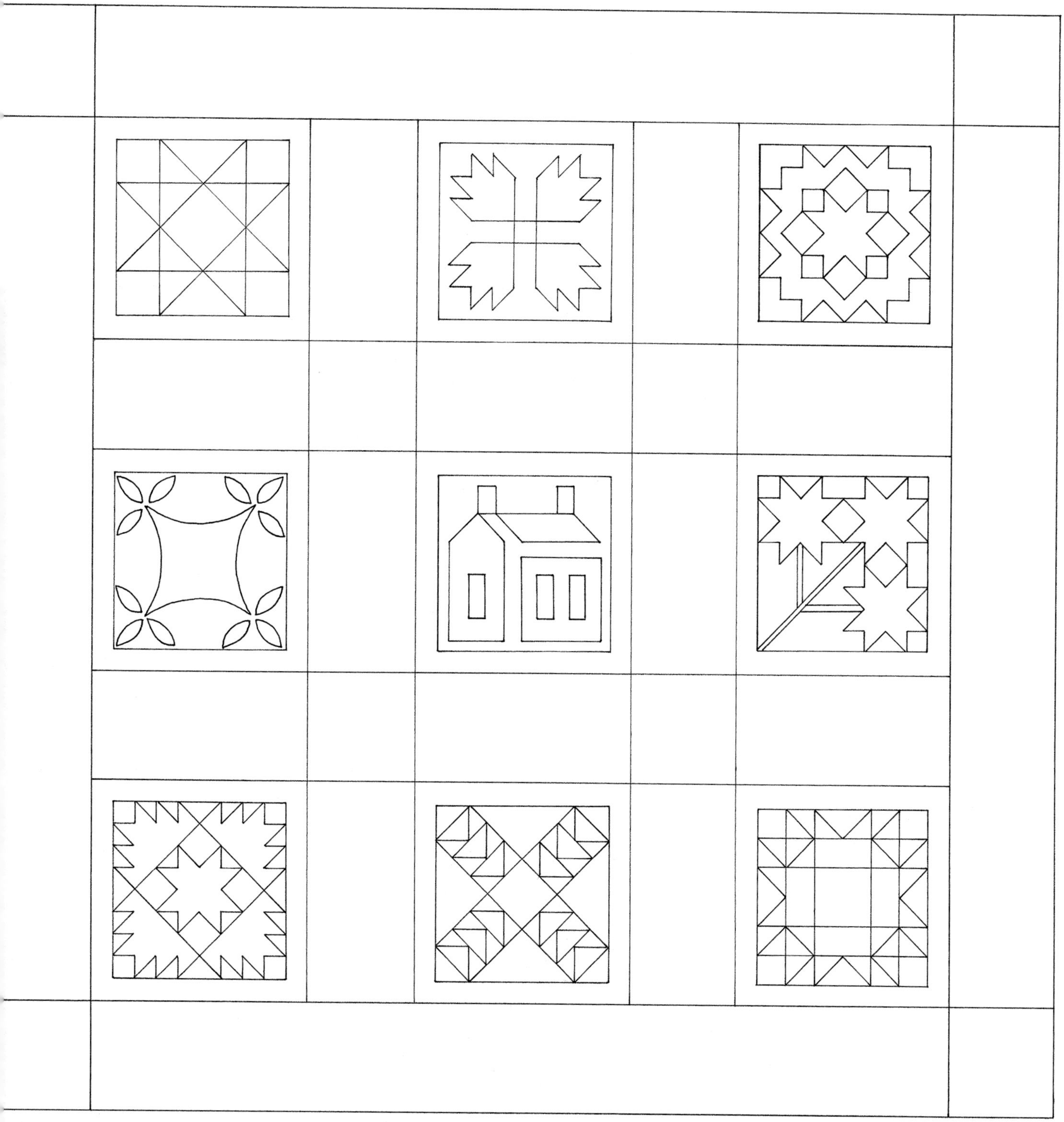

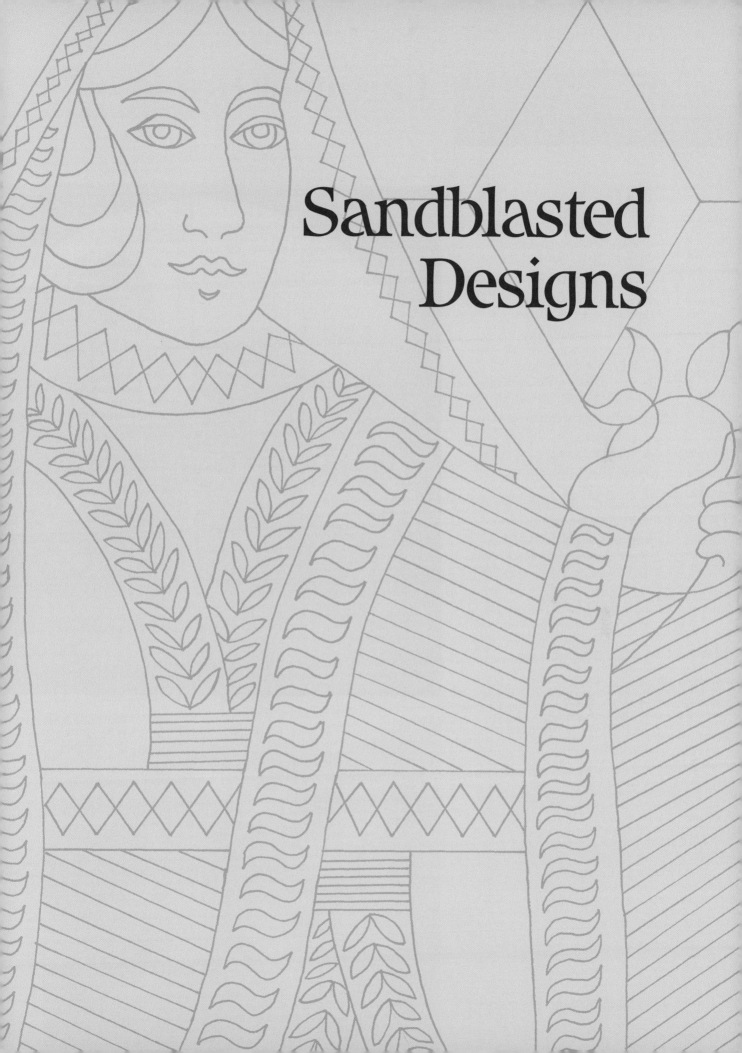

Sandblasted
Designs

Carousel Horse

27 1/2 x 27 1/2 inches

While browsing in a bookstore, I found a wonderful book about carousels, which inspired this design. I loved making all the details by sandblasting both flashed and transparent glass. The detail on the yellow pole was sandblasted into a transparent yellow glass, and it remained yellow because I didn't use flashed glass. I achieved some shading in the blue saddle blanket because I used a dark transparent glass, not flashed glass, and deeply sandblasted one edge of the scallop pattern; however, I had to be careful not to blast too deep or the glass would become fragile. To create the yellow fringe on the blanket, I used a wood burner to cut lines in contact paper on the glass and then sandblasted it. All the details on both flashed and transparent glass would have been impossible with traditional methods of stained glass. The background circle is a clear Cotswold glass, and a cobalt-blue glass border keeps it all together. Notice how a few details extend into the blue border.

King of Spades

16 x 25 inches

This design is one of the reasons I learned to sandblast glass. I wanted to be able to add all that detail. I have played a lot of card games, including bridge, so the King of Spades was a natural (the king is the top face card and spades is the top suit). I used clear contact paper to cover all the glass pieces that were sandblasted, cut the designs with a knife, and then sandblasted the color off the flashed glass. On transparent glass, like the face, I drew the design on paper, laid the glass with clear contact paper on that, and cut it out. On darker colors, when I couldn't see the design through the glass, I traced the design onto the contact paper and then cut it out. The face and hands were cut from clear window glass. I felt the patterns on these pieces were complex enough that the glass needed to be smooth, with no texture.

Queen of Diamonds

16¼ x 25 inches

After making the King of Spades, I decided to make a queen. Again, the face and hands were made from window glass, with the design sandblasted into them. For some of her clothes, I covered the glass with clear contact paper and used a wood burner and metal ruler to cut the lines into it. When sandblasted, this created the straight-lined pattern. I used the same glass for this panel as the king so they made a matching pair.